For Sally

Malcolm Fryer
Evocations

"I must go down to the seas again, for the call of the running tide

Is a wild call and a clear call that may not be denied;

And all I ask is a windy day with the white clouds flying,

And the flung spray and the blown spume, and the sea gulls crying."

Sea Fever by John Masefield

Opposite: Fingal's Cave, Oil on canvas, 40" x 50"

To step in front of a Malcolm Fryer painting is to be blown away by a salty gale with the crying of seabirds in your ears, or to find peace in blue-green water jewelled with fish or in the soft lush recesses of a secret garden. The broad sweep of subject matter and vivid colour arrest the eye and draw it in not just to one world but to the juxtaposition of two: one well known and well understood to the eye and conscious level of thought; the other strange yet hauntingly familiar. It is this latter element which constitutes the essence of Malcolm's craft: it smacks you between the eyes - to quote an astonished art critic in 1967 - and awakens the senses, evoking in the viewer's mind images of those equally well known but often less well understood places of the heart. These powerful evocations of the other world we all inhabit translate the scars and balm of our lives into colour and texture. A recognisable horizon might be depicted in a cherry red light which infuses the ruffled sea below; majestic trees arch over what appears to be a spiritual retreat; the Turneresque brushstrokes of a sun shower are slashed in violent contemporary colour. These other-worldly and often restless patterns reflect the moods of an artist who has observed these scenes many, many times and who is still observing.

Opposite: The Flying Dutchman,
Oil on canvas, 40" x 50"

Malcolm's quest to portray the physical and psychological environment that man battles to harness began out on the stretches of the Lancashire and Yorkshire moors, it continued on the east coast of Scotland, and after a break of several years now focuses on not only the vistas of our northwest and northeast coasts but also fresh and equally vibrant themes such as forest glades and underwater tableaux – a profusion of colour in a more closed environment, providing a calmer contrast to the wild open seascapes and grasslands.

Early successes after his first major exhibition in 1962 have ensured that Malcolm's work has been widely exhibited in this country and is also represented in private and public collections both here and abroad.

In 2004 Art-Amis near Hitchin in Hertfordshire took Malcolm under its wing to arrange a variety of unusual and exciting venues in which to display his work, combining a modern approach to exhibiting works of art with good old-fashioned hospitality whereby the viewer has the opportunity to meet the artist in a relaxed atmosphere – a most appropriate way to promote an artist like Malcolm who combines traditional values with a modern feel, and who himself once sought a novel approach to curating works of art. Art-Amis represents several exciting artists whose bold, distinctive styles show us the very best in contemporary art.

The Wave, Oil on canvas, 27" x 33"

Lighthouse, Oil on canvas, 40" x 50"

The Old Pier, Oil on canvas, 22" x 31"

Previous page: Sea Fever, Oil on canvas, 50" x 40"

Malcolm was born in Manchester in 1937 and grew up in Blackburn, Lancashire, and encouragement to pursue his future career came early. The son of an architect who worked for the local authority and in his spare time played the organ in church and took a sketchbook with him on family holidays, the young Malcolm was shaped by the awe in which his father held natural and man-made forms and by his love of powerful music. At the age of four or five he was given a set of stone building bricks with which he built a fantasy cathedral to his father's design, and a few years later he would regularly take himself off on family holidays with his own sketchbook. One early artistic endeavour was drawing the tower of Canterbury Cathedral while fuelling himself on currant buns from a local shop and thinking, "This is it!" He remembers his first set of Winsor & Newton oils, used for his first effort on canvas to portray a defunct fountain filled in with soil and now planted with flowers. At the age of twelve a bout of illness unexpectedly ensured the sale of his first painting, when the doctor was distracted by his painting of the canal by Grimshaw Park, and for which he was prepared to pay the princely sum of £5. In 1959, after some initial training at Blackburn School of Art, Malcolm was awarded a local authority grant to attend the Lancaster School of Art where students were instructed to examine the innovative work of American expressionists such as Jackson Pollock and Mark Rothko.

This left a lasting influence on Malcolm, who was also struck particularly by the stark landscape painting of David Bomberg.

Unwilling after college to attempt to survive in a garret on ideas and principles, he acquired a teaching post at a tough secondary modern in Salford along with the unwelcome advice to take with him a gymshoe to keep order. During his two years there Malcolm found encouragement to be the more effective learning aid, even though this led alarmingly on one occasion to a couple of over-eager pupils bringing into his sculpture class a piece of marble stolen from the local cemetery. He rejoiced in the enthusiasm he saw around him and the naïve art he saw produced and, finding himself also in the role of pottery teacher, welcomed the opportunity to teach himself as well as his pupils a new craft!

In the meantime Malcolm was honing his skills with his own painting and had already had his work exhibited along with that of other Northern artists in Blackburn and Lancaster. He recalls the occasion he set off during this period to see a Turner exhibition at the Royal Academy, and being advised to start not with "all that boring brown stuff" but from the other end, the section which demonstrated the master's use of bright watercolour and the timeless quality of his later works. Malcolm acted on this advice, and the thrill of this experience has stayed with him all his life.

Land Yachts, Oil on canvas, 40" x 50"

Opposite: On Golden Seas, Oil on canvas, 12" x 16"

Loverly Liverpool, Oil on card, 20" x 29"

Opposite: Towards the Dusk, Oil on canvas, 39" x 39"

A major breakthrough came in June 1962 with a hugely successful exhibition, sponsored by Guinness, of ground-breaking abstract art by four local artists including Malcolm at the Art Gallery of Lancaster Storey Institute. A reporter from The Visitor remarked that "most of the visitors on the opening night appeared to me to be wondering just what they were looking for", despite one helpful young lady's advice to stand back from each painting and look deeper into it, but the reporter conceded that he could "appreciate the colour". However, a visitor who came away impressed during the setting up of the exhibition was one David Hockney. Proof of the power of Malcolm's art was in the invitation he now received to be appointed visiting lecturer at the Blackpool School of Art, a position he was honoured to hold for the next ten years. Malcolm continued to paint, teaming up with another artist to tour several English universities in order to exhibit, market and sell their work with what proved to be a high degree of success.

Selling prices ranged from £15 to £45 a piece, with the option of hiring a piece at £1 a month, these fees being deducted from the original figure in the event of eventual purchase. With a family to support on what was at one point £25 a month, this was hard but rewarding work. Malcolm enjoyed his first solo exhibition around this time, at Birmingham University.

Afternoons Calm, Mixed Media, 22" x 30"

Sea Study, Oil on card, 11" x 22"

What with pictures in private collections in London, Penrith, Preston and in the Arthur Guinness and Provincial Insurance collections, his status now of founder member of the Northern Artists' Action Group, and a TV appearance as Granada's "Artist of the Month", Malcolm's career as an artist was assured.

One review of his work in the Grundy House, South Shore exhibition in 1967 described his delivery as a "frontal assault", using "colour like ammunition" in such pieces as "Yellow Fall", "Moors Summer" and "Blackshape".

In his solo exhibition at the Lewis Textile Museum, Blackburn, the pictures – all titled "Landscape" – showed clearly the classic Fryer touch: a series of oil paintings and drawings on a theme rather than a particular place, all the result of a far greater volume of work discarded in the process of capturing what was in this case the rugged atmosphere of moorland and the patterns of sky and rock. Monoprints and collages also featured in the exhibition, with yellow a predominant colour – as it continues to be today.

In 1967 Malcolm was appointed curator of the prestigious Haworth Art Gallery, Accrington, where he devoted the following three years to the rewarding challenge of not only staging exhibitions for other artists but also promoting such events in other ways by organising musical evenings, inviting a number of poets, John Ogden among them, and providing refreshment for the many people who came from far and near. Exhibits were not limited to paintings: materials ranged from engravings to perspex, and Malcolm was instrumental in saving the Gallery's priceless collection of Tiffany favrile glass from being shipped back to America. New art was constantly encouraged, whether in the form of an open-air sculpture show or an open exhibition for locals including children. Malcolm was also intrumental in helping to form local art associations such as the Mid-Pennine Association for the Arts in Burnley, and in staging under the directorship of Liverpool artist and poet Adrian Henry the Second Eleven exhibition of local artists – including Lennon and McCartney – whose submissions to a major exhibition at a prestigious Liverpool gallery around this time had been refused in favour of the more fashionable London artists.

A new phase in Malcolm's life came with a move up to Arbroath on the east coast of Scotland in the 1970s in order to take up the position of warden at Hospitalfield House, whose board of principals comprised the governors of Scotland's four major art schools in Edinburgh, Glasgow, Aberdeen and Dundee, with Robert Philipson in the chair. Guest artists included Carel Weight, Professor of Art at the Royal College whose passion was to encourage other artists, and Peter Blake, one of Britain's foremost pop artists best known for designing the Sergeant Pepper album sleeve for the Beatles. During these years Malcolm found the different coastal scenery a fresh source of inspiration, and he produced many images of the area including " Beyond Auchmithie", now in the permanent collection in the Atkinson Art Gallery, Southport. These pieces were saved to be shown in England on his return there, in one case resulting in a sell-out exhibition at the Vernon Gallery in Preston. In a glowing review of the work on display at the Great Hage Gallery in Rivington, reporter Carol Kroch described the viewer's experience as "a voyage into the land of discovery … [the landscapes] engage the imagination as more precise conventionally pretty scenes and abstraction for its own sake do not".

Despite his successes, and like so many artists who do not paint those conventionally pretty scenes for easier money, Malcolm simply could not make ends meet on his painting alone after his time in Arbroath, and on his return south decided to pursue a new avenue which was still in some way connected to the world of art and also that of his past: the antique business.

Beyond Auchmithie, Oil on canvas, 36" x 48"

A friend of his father's, the owner of Broadbents & Boothroyds Department Store in Southport and great supporter of the arts, Tony Pedlar, took a grateful Malcolm under his wing by organising rent-free warehouse premises in a shop in the Victorian Arcade and setting him up with a collection of antiques. This gesture proved profitable for Malcolm in more ways than one over the following fifteen years, for he now found himself able to indulge his passion for beautiful furniture and to find new outlets for selling his paintings, while choosing at this time – because of tragedy in his life – to take a complete break from painting.

In the same way that the antiques business put a complete stop to the painting, so in turn the recession that ensued after several years prompted Malcolm to paint his way out of it and thereby back in many ways to his old life. By now he was happily remarried, and after a spell of living and painting in Appleby ("Castle Keep" being an example of his work there), he returned to Southport. He set out with renewed energy to capture on canvas the subject matter that had defined his early days: the wilds of the northwest, the cityscape of Liverpool with its imposing cathedral, the wave-lashed piers and wheeling gulls, boats on a winter's day, and two series of paintings known as "The Storm". Each vaulted sky and rough-hewn object revealed the robust architectural influence of Malcolm's youth and his fascination with stained glass framed in black leads. One particularly encouraging success was an exhibition at the Oddfellows Gallery in Prince Charlie's House, Kendal in 1996.

... He was o'er powered
By Nature: by the turbulence subdued
Of his own mind; by mystery and hope,
And the first virgin passion of a soul
Communing with the glorious universe.

Full often wished he that the winds might rage
When they were silent : far more fondly now
Than in his earlier season did he love
Tempestuous nights - the conflict and the sounds
That live in darkness.

The Excursion - The Wanderer by William Wordsworth

Opposite: Landscapes Edge, Oil on canvas, 36" x 48"

Emerald Bay, Oil on card, 13" x 16"

Opposite: Castle Keep, Oil on canvas, 39" x 39"

Craig Bancroft at Northcote Manor

There were additional and unexpected sources of inspiration too. A commission from a designer friend to paint some bold tulips in a Gauguinesque style led to a series of such paintings now housed at Northcote Manor Hotel in the Ribble Valley. For the past decade Northcote Manor has considered a Malcolm Fryer painting to be as excellent local produce as the food they serve, and his works are displayed accordingly in the hotel restaurant to enhance the diners' experience. Chef Nigel Haworth, with his joint proprietor Craig Bancroft has commissioned Malcolm to provide two special pictures to reflect the ambience of the Manor and perhaps to design a special Northcote Manor plate.

The outdoor idyll cultivated by Malcolm's keen gardener wife Sally, complete with its bird bath and the feel of her calm influence, prompted the first of two garden series in soft mysterious tones reminiscent of Manet. In 2000 Malcolm travelled to Berwick-upon-Tweed to explore once again the light on the east coast and to produce some fresh work. In addition to these projects, two years later he and his sculptor son Simon staged a joint exhibition at his old stamping ground, Haworth Art Gallery.

At this stage, almost as if to boost the strength of the work being produced, further ups and downs ensued in Malcolm's life. He was able to take up full time painting in 1998 but suffered an even greater tragedy just a few years later with Sally's death, after which he experienced an outpouring of work from the adrenalin of shock.

Malcolm continues to search for new horizons while returning time after time to his old haunts in the northwest. A visit to the Caribbean in the spring of 2004 was a new departure for Malcolm in more ways than one, for this was his first experience of long-distance travel as well as of the very different light and foliage. The time spent in the luxuriant grounds of Harmony Hall, a hide-away on the unspoilt coastline of Antigua, inspired a series of drawings and paintings in hot and unfamiliar violets, sapphires, emeralds and turquoises. In typical Fryer fashion these do not depict scenes as such, apart from the remains of an old harbour, but the profound effect of this visit invigorated Malcolm's work both there and on his return home .

Antiguan Landscape, Mixed Media, 33" x 38"

Light on the Estuary, Watercolour, 33" x 38"

Jolly Harbour, Watercolour, 33" x 38"

Opposite:
Paradise Palm, Mixed Media, 21" x 31"

West Indian Resting Place, Watercolour, 31" x 38"

Serenity put out to Sea, Oil on canvas, 40" x 60"

Previous page: Morning Star, Oil on canvas, 36" x 48"

There are new horizons closer at hand too. Malcolm has executed a cathedral series and a further garden series. A field full of yellow rape near Ely calls to him each time he drives by. A Hertfordshire pond and an exquisite Tiffany glass vase dating from 1890 have provided the impetus for the more recent fish series.

The direct result of having closely observed and handled the vase while curator at Haworth, in order to admire the revolutionary effect of it being full of water and swimming fish, produced a vast painting called "Tiffany Fish". A new commission is to paint the crypt in St Paul's Cathedral, a challenge for which Malcolm is preparing by turning to Turner's Petworth interiors. Yet Malcolm is not content only to portray light, water and form in all their mystery. He is seeking to paint sound too, one obsession of his being the thrashing of the elements around Fingal's Cave.

Despite such creativity, Malcolm also produces on occasion more representational work, for like many others he literally cannot afford to delve more deeply than he does into more obscure avenues of his art. He is careful, however, not to compromise his integrity, for he cannot paint what he cannot feel.

It is a case of eking a living from other means too, such as teaching here and there; he has been enjoying his annual visits as guest artist at Liverpool High School for the past few years, and he holds talks and workshops for various art societies. There is the occasional exhibition too, such as one held in Liverpool at the time of the fuel shortages in 2000 when the stranded and frustrated locals thronged in front of his pictures and proceeded to get drunk – an unforeseen event which resulted in a more successful (and sober) exhibition at the city's Hanover Galleries.

Sea-painter and poet, a weaver of dreams,
Elemental translator of abstract extremes,
Designer, creator, green-demons of art,
Whip storm-inspirations to salt-lash my heart

The painter is watching; the poet he hears
The song of the humpback, the wave-dragon nears
And roars of the fate of the philistine man
Sucked back to the dark where the circle began.

Jean M Thomas

Nature's Jewel, Mixed Media, 21" x 28"

The Delamere Pond Series

30

Malcolm's restless search to portray what he feels is reflected in his working methods. He executes rough drawings, he takes occasional photographs strictly for reference, but it is his memory and mood which do the donkey work as he frequently passes – deliberately or by chance - through each chosen place. The work often takes months and even years to develop, and one picture can lead on to another area. For every painting produced there are two more that are thrown away; and for every painting on the easel there are easily fifty or sixty more in the pipeline as he shifts his gaze from one to another. Malcolm does not produce a particular number of workable paintings and drawings to order for any one exhibition; rather he works on dozens all the time on rotation.

"This is a calling, not a profession," he explains. "I simply have to do it."
And this is a calling which does not rely on the muse taking him. Malcolm relies instead on discipline and hard graft, getting his hours in even when not in the mood. He eschews the idea of drug-enhancing activity as much as he does the muse: "The odd bottle of wine at night is pleasant, but only after the work is done. Working under the influence is disastrous; you're not in control!"

For all his dissatisfaction and frenzied activity, Malcolm points out that his approach is not as extreme as that of another expressionist he admires, the extraordinary French painter Chaim Soutine who in the 1920s found fame and fortune enough to buy back his earlier unconventional and passionate compositions of sides of meat in order to destroy the lot. Malcolm understands that mindset however.

"Painting is like a football," he says. "Until the ball moves, nothing happens."
Churning out the same type of work one is most comfortable with might be cosy and profitable for some, but for Malcolm it would only mean boredom and the loss of integrity.

Opposite: Sea Defence, Mixed Media, 33" x 23"

Arcadian Study 1, Mixed Media, 17" x 24"

Arcadian Study 2, Mixed Media, 17" x 24"

Opposite:
Arcadian Twilight, Oil on canvas, 40" x 40"

33

Discipline, application and a distinctive style constitute the anchor for living with life's changes, changes not just in terms of the ups and downs and exploring fresh avenues but also in terms of one's age, the time of year and particular events. Malcolm no longer does as much outdoor painting as in his younger years, nor is he as prolific as he once was, preferring nowadays to get a smaller number of efforts more spot on. He points out too that it takes years to learn painting techniques, and the learning never stops. The change over to summertime is productive: not surprisingly, Malcolm gets up with the sun.

When tragedy has hit, as has happened several times, he has found painting to be a solace. At times of financial hardship, necessity is the mother of invention. On those occasions when canvases were too expensive to buy, card was the cheaper option – and on discovering how much he enjoyed working with oils on card, Malcolm was even more delighted when he realised Turner had done the same. Malcolm has been prepared to paint on anything. Bits of scrap wood have served their purpose, sand has been added to bulk up paint, and Abbot Hall in Kendal has a piece of his work which was daubed on the side of a packing case. A recent long spell without a studio prompted Malcolm to work in mixed media, with acrylic the new medium favoured for its functionality.

Opposite: At Rest, Oil on canvas, 30" x 48"

Malcolm has a studio once again, this time in a neighbouring garage, but it doesn't do to be too solitary. He repairs to the living area in the kitchen when need be so that he can enjoy his daughter Katie's company and allow her to boss him about and clean up the mess from his labours.

While he has at hand various media including charcoal, pastels, watercolours, acrylics and oils, Malcolm's preferences are for drawing ("sometimes I love drawing even more than painting, and my exhibitions always have a mix of the two") and for working in oils which give the depth and richness needed for his textured painting. Malcolm explains that the idea is to get the paint on the canvas and let it play. "It's not enough just to throw the paint, but it's a wonderful start."

His work is imbued with romance. The impressionistic treatment of light combined with explosive expressionist colours show nature's fickle moods to be those of our own: of violence, unease, solitude and peace.

The strong, soaring music of composers such as Beethoven and Wagner is Malcolm's other passion while he is working. It provides the perfect sound setting for his seascapes, arcadian forest clearings and ashen shores. Yellows, blues and blacks often predominate in the palette, although the blacks more so in younger days than now; they fuse warmth from the golden rays with the clear emptiness of the blues, both being tempered by the harsh paint of the ridges on sea and land.

Electricity out to Sea, Mixed Media, 23" x 33"

Ocean Colour Scene, Oil on canvas, 16" x 60"

New Skies, Oil on canvas, 16" x 60"

Overleaf: Tranquil Summer Dawn,
Oil on canvas, 40" x 60"

Carol Kroch, Art critic of The Guardian's description of Malcolm's style of painting is a good pointer:

"The artist appears to employ two manners simultaneously. In one, he deploys a matt application of paint in separate colour fields: sky and greenery interspersed by a patch of daffodils; striated sky and shore. More usually, the surface is richly encrusted and glazed with powerful strokes traversing the canvas, where mighty trees converge as they dip into bracken, and bleeding Turneresque gold masks a vermilion sun."

"The sky and sea are God's creation," Malcolm says. "I have been trying to get near to portraying them all my life." The constant battle for him is to express their beauty and wonder while avoiding the chocolate box effect.

Strong simple shapes give structure to the more loose and emotional handling of paint. The drawings of Henry Moore and the childlike creations of Paul Klee have both had an influence in Malcolm's life.

The sense of awe and fascination for things both spiritual and architectural that Malcolm gained from his father have stayed with him all his life and inspired him in dark times. The tall curved lines of his cathedral pictures, outlined by a radiance beyond, might be the arches of a stained glass window or the boughs of a stately column of trees.

You can see this stained glass quality with its jewel-like colours elsewhere, in the reflections on the night waves of "Morning Star" and on the crackled expanse of "Electricity Out To Sea", and there is a vision of true glory in "Prospect of Peace" where seabirds whirl in a vortex of lilac light – evidence of the new Fryer palette from his West Indies visit, and evidence of his continual pushing.

While few of these works can be identified in terms of place, they are quintessentially English after years of study of the rising of the sun on the east coast and its setting on the west. The impressions gained in the tropics have served to inform Malcolm's work back home, contributing, as he declares, to his image of Southport! A successor of Malcolm's at the Haworth Art Gallery has described his painting as being in the grand English landscape tradition of Constable and Turner.

Malcolm's purpose is to transport the viewer to another world and discover something that strikes a chord. In the same way that Malcolm returns again and again to a place and a piece of work in progress, so the viewer is rewarded by returning to observe – not just to look – at the same piece. Malcolm seeks to encourage, not to tell the viewer what to see there, and different viewings may evoke different responses.

Prospect of Peace, Oil on canvas, 39" x 39"

The mission to encourage others has been paramount for one who himself pursues a difficult calling. Malcolm says that he has been blessed along the way, what with the parental encouragement he received, the grant which admitted him to the Lancaster School of Art, the sponsorship offered by Guinness, the glow of limelight he experienced when the actress Dame Edith Evans bought one of his works, the assistance given to set up in the antiques business, and not least the loyal support provided by family including his daughter Juliet and her husband who are a constant presence at exhibitions, and by galleries, buyers, and now Art-Amis. This encouragement is in fact patronage, the sort that was invaluable to Turner. In seeking to give what he has received, Malcolm has taught in schools and workshops, seen his son follow in his footsteps, and represented and encouraged other artists through his own curating. It was fitting that one recent exhibition arranged through Art-Amis took place at a preparatory school known for promoting the arts, where Malcolm and his fellow artists had the opportunity to spend a day leading workshops for the pupils.

In turn, these various ways of encouraging others have helped inform Malcolm's own work. He remembers and acknowledges the naïve art of his young secondary modern pupils, the intriguing design of the Tiffany glass vase in his care, the striking form of the furniture in his antiques gallery.

Malcolm is delighted to see the trend once again for people to want works of art adorning their own homes, and is grateful to such companies and individuals as Saatchi & Saatchi for helping to revive and promote this interest, thereby giving a number of painters today the opportunity to make a living from what they do best.

"There has been so much ignorance around," he says, sadly but fondly recalling the time he was asked by a gallery visitor which painter had most influenced him, and on hearing the name Turner then asked if Malcolm had met him.

Opposite: The Deluge, Oil on card, 15" x 22"   *Overleaf: Smugglers, Oil on canvas, 40" x 50"*

Plunders Moon
Oil on canvas
16" x 12"

The Wreckers
Oil on canvas
16" x 12"

47

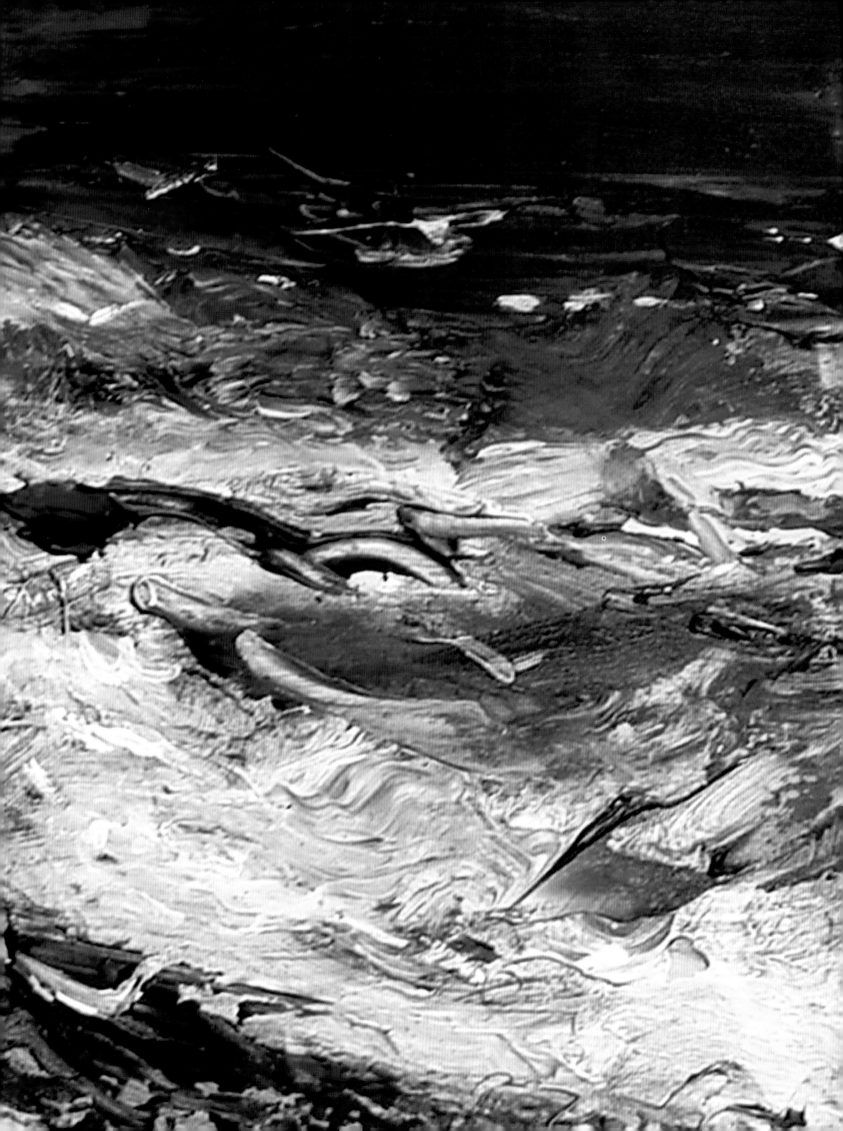

The past three years have seen sales of well over a hundred paintings, a fact which is testimony to ongoing success, and Malcolm feels the best works do come later in life. For him the joy of selling his work never diminishes, in part because he can look to buying the next canvas but also – and more importantly – because he has communicated to the buyer his simple yet profound message which demands a response.

Malcolm is glad not to have had the opportunity to buy back and destroy past works the way Soutine did, because he feels genuine pleasure on seeing an old friend on a wall in a good home. His fervent hope is that at least one of these works will last a lifetime or more, in the manner of a Beethoven symphony. Another old friend for Malcolm is Blackburn itself, and the major 2006 exhibition there, and in Southport, marks Malcolm's return to his roots after 35 years.

Malcolm is philosophical about his life and work. "It's a cliché," he told The Lancashire Evening Telegraph reporter Ann Chadwick in an interview in March 2005, "but artists have to struggle in a sense. You have to make your work better and better. If I had had instant success I might have lost integrity. I've only scratched the surface [with my work]. Artists have to have humility. We can only do a tiny bit. That's my philosophy, this constant search."

This search, he adds, signifies his continual aspiration to paint the ultimate peaceful horizon. For an artist whose work has been described by The Daily Telegraph as "charged with colour and emotion" with "a strong vein of music running through his work", the most apt title would be that of romantic expressionist. Using modern techniques to evoke a timeless world, Malcolm puts into brushstrokes what the rest of us simply feel.

Two voices are there; one is of the sea,
One of the mountains ; each a mighty voice:
In both from age to age, thou didst rejoice,
They were thy chosen music, liberty!

Thought of a Briton, Sonnets by William Wordsworth

Previous page: Tempest Tide, Oil on canvas, 20" x 16"

Douglas, Mixed Media, 20" x 26"

Study for Yacht Race 1, Mixed Media, 22" x 29"

Study for Yacht Race 2, Mixed Media, 22" x 29"   *Opposite: Yacht Race, Oil on canvas, 40" x 50"*

Haven, Oil on canvas, 40" x 50"

Previous page: Cathedral Study 1998, Oil on card, 14" x 14"
Solace in Sanctuary, Oil on board, 32" x 24"

Malcolm Fryer's work has been exhibited at the Blackburn Art Gallery, Bolton Art Gallery, Lewis Textile Museum (Blackburn), Atkinson Art Gallery (Southport), Vernon Gallery (Preston), Great Hage Gallery (Rivington), Grundy House (Blackpool), Merida Gallery (Louisville, U.S.A.), Milan, The Broeckman (Chester), Oddfellows (Kendal), Abbot Hall Art Gallery (Kendal), Hanover Galleries (Liverpool), St Martin's College (Lancaster), Downs Gallery (Altrincham), Ribchester Roman Museum, Brown's (Newcastle), Eclipse Gallery (Hitchin), the Universities of Birmingham, Bristol, Hull, Keele, Leeds, Liverpool, York and Warwick, and various Hertfordshire venues including Auberge du Lac, Redcoats Hotel, Heath Mount School, Haileybury College, the Porsche Centre in Hatfield and Sheene Mill, Cambridgeshire.

He is permanently represented in many public and private collections, including the Blackburn and Bolton Art Galleries, Northcote Manor (Blackburn), Salford Education Committee, Provincial Insurance Ltd, The Atkinson Art Gallery, Southport, Granada Television, Arthur Guinness (Park Royal) Ltd, Liverpool Health Authority, Daniel Thwaites Ltd, Broadbent's Southport Ltd, Southport and Formby Hospital Trust, the Universities of Leeds and Liverpool and in many collections in this country, Europe, the USA and Australia.

Listed in Twentieth Century Painters and Sculptors, Vol VI by Frances Spalding.

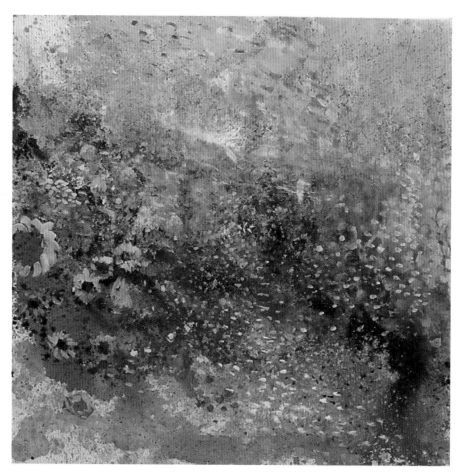

Summer Song 1
Oil on canvas, 40" x 40"

Summer Song 2
Oil on canvas, 40" x 40"

Opposite: The Secret Garden, Oil on canvas, 48" x 36"

Angus Landscape, Oil on canvas, 36" x 48"

Opposite: Boiling Sea, Acrylic on canvas, 28" x 36"

Light Dark Reeds, Oil on canvas, 32" x 40"

Winter Shore, Oil on card, 13" x 30"

Song of Sunrise, Oil on Canvas ,24" x 32"

ACKNOWLEDGEMENTS

Art-Amis would like to acknowledge the enthusiastic support of the
following, some of whose paintings are featured in this publication:

Nigel Haworth and Craig Bancroft at Northcote Manor; David and Helena Hodgins; Mike and Christine Cleasby;
Mark and Emily Dixon; Trevor and Janice Norwood; Debbie Daniel; Marcel and Margriet Velterop;
Mike and Liz Wells; Mike and Jayne Bradley-Russell; Evelyn Tweedlie; Andy and Jan Turner; Uta Coutts;
Robert and Gilly Chelsom; Darrell and Fiona Beck; Sean Larrangton-White; Steven Saunders at Sheene Mill;
Valerie Waters; Carolyn Knight; Karen Hammond; Mr Lauchlan and Miss Davidson; Rob Rayward;
Alan and Karen Brown; Joy Saunders; Mr Barlow; Mark and Kim Cherry; Ian and Victoria Croft;
Jonathan and Carolyn Marsh; Mr and Mrs Purver; Mr and Mrs Stacy;
Thelma Stoller; Dr and Mrs Wallis; Mr and Mrs Nash; Stella Walkey;Ruth Waring; Mrs Taffs; Caroline Yeldham;
Jim and Lesley Knight;Alistair Hay; Fred and Joan McAdam; Mr and Mrs R Cook; Len and Karen Williamson
Professor and Mrs Slater; Mr and Mrs Harris; Carol Cox; Mr M Walker;Redcoats Farmhouse, Auberge du Lac,
and Riccardo and Marilisa Parisi at Harmony Hall, Antigua and any other Malcolm Fryer collectors

The publishers would also like to thank The Society of Authors as the Literary Representative of the
Estate of John Masefield for their permission to publish an extract from "Sea Fever"
Despite all attempts it has been impossible to trace the original copyright owner of the poem by Jean M Thomas

Beyond Auchmithie reproduced by kind permission of
Sefton MBC Leisure Services Department,
Arts and Cultural Services, Atkinson Art Gallery
Landscapes Edge and Angus Landscape reproduced
by kind permission of Blackburn Museum and Art Gallery

**Malcolm Fryer
Evocations**

First published in Great Britain in 2007 by:
Art-Amis
The Stables, Delamere House
Great Wymondley
Near Hitchin, Hertfordshire
SG4 7ER

Page Layout by Scott Tierney
Editorial by Victoria Jackson

ISBN   978 -0 -9554214 -0 -2